Good Manners
with Your Parents

by Rebecca Felix

illustrated by Gary LaCoste

visit us at www.abdopublishing.com

Published by Magic Wagon, a division of the ABDO Group, PO Box 398166, Minneapolis, MN, 55439. Copyright © 2014 by Abdo Consulting Group, Inc. International copyrights reserved in all countries. All rights reserved. No part of this book may be reproduced in any form without written permission from the publisher.

Looking Glass Library™ is a trademark and logo of Magic Wagon.

Printed in the United States of America, North Mankato, Minnesota.
102013
012014
 The book contains at least 10% recycled materials.

Text by Rebecca Felix
Illustrations by Gary LaCoste
Edited by Stephanie Hedlund and Rochelle Baltzer
Interior layout and design by Renée LaViolette
Cover design by Renée LaViolette

Library of Congress Cataloging-in-Publication Data

Felix, Rebecca, 1984-
  Good manners with your parents / by Rebecca Felix ; illustrated by Gary LaCoste.
    pages cm. -- (Good manners in relationships)
  Includes index.
  ISBN 978-1-62402-026-1
  1. Etiquette for children and teenagers--Juvenile literature. 2. Parent and child--Juvenile literature. I. LaCoste, Gary, illustrator. II. Title.
  BJ1857.C5F37185 2014
  395.1'22--dc23
                                    2013030852

Contents

Why Do Good Manners Matter with Parents?

Joe is eating cereal before school. Joe's mom asked him to rinse his bowl when he is done. She also asked him to feed the dog.

Joe finishes his cereal. He thinks about what his mom asked. But Joe wants to watch cartoons before the bus arrives. Should he leave the bowl on the table and go watch television? Or should Joe rinse the bowl and feed the dog?

5

Joe should rinse his bowl. Then, he should feed the dog. This shows good manners. By doing what his mother asked, Joe will show he can follow directions. Following directions shows good manners. Good manners are an important part of your relationship with your parents.

Always clean up after yourself, even when your parents do not ask. This shows parents consideration.

What would relationships with parents be like
without good manners? Joe might leave his bowl
on the table. He might skip feeding the dog. Or,
he might give the dog his cereal bowl of leftover
milk instead of dog food! This could cause a mess.
Joe's mom might get upset. And Joe might get into
trouble and become upset, too.

9

Show Good Manners with Parents!

Showing parents good manners makes relationships better. Respect is a base of good manners with parents. This means treating parents how you would like to be treated. Showing parents respect tells them you care about their feelings. What other manners are important with parents?

Stepparents should be shown the same respect as birth parents.

It is good manners to listen to your parents. Follow their rules. Parents often set rules to keep kids safe.

Joe's parents have a rule about knives. Joe and his brother Brett must ask before using knives. Brett wants to slice an apple. He should ask his mom or dad for help. Or, he should ask for permission to use a knife. This will show Brett's parents he listens. It will show he respects what they say.

It is good manners to speak politely to your parents. Talking rudely does not help you get along with them. It shows bad manners. Think of how you talk to other adults. You should show your parents the same respect. Talking to them politely includes using something called "magic words."

Joe's favorite television show is about to start. But his dad is watching the news. There is a polite way Joe can ask his dad to switch programs. He should use the word "please." This shows good manners when asking a parent for something. "Please" is a magic word that makes parents more likely to do something for you.

Magic words are short and easy to remember. Using them makes talking with parents more pleasant!

When Joe's dad agrees to switch programs, Joe should say "thank you." These are a set of magic words. When a parent agrees to do something you ask, always say "thank you."

It is also polite to thank parents for things they provide for you. This includes making you dinner, buying you clothes, or planning your birthday party. Telling parents "thank you" shows them you appreciate these things.

Parents should thank kids for doing nice things, too. When parents say "thank you," the polite reply is "you're welcome."

Everyone has a bad day sometimes. Even parents!
Sometimes parents get sick. Or they are very busy.
Being kind to parents in these situations shows
good manners.

What if Joe told his mom her new haircut was ugly?
Or if Brett got upset that his dad missed his softball
game because of work? Their parents might feel
bad. Acting this way does not show good manners.
Now get ready to see some good manners in
motion!

Manners in Motion

Brett and Joe are going out to dinner with their parents. On the drive, their mom asks them to follow some rules.

"Please use your napkins at the restaurant," she says. "And be polite to the server."

"Okay, Mom!" Brett and Joe say.

At the restaurant, Joe and Brett eat all of their dinner. The server returns to their table.

"Dessert for anyone?" she asks.

"Can we please order ice cream?" Joe asks their parents. They say it is okay.

"Thank you!" Joe and Brett say. They order politely.

The server brings the ice cream. Joe and Brett thank her and dig in. Their dad asks for a bite. He takes a scoop. But it spills on his shirt! Brett and Joe want to laugh. But their dad looks upset. The ice cream left a stain.

"Here is my napkin, Dad," says Joe. "I hope the stain comes out!" Their dad smiles and reaches for another bite.

How did Joe and Brett show their parents good manners? They listened and followed directions. They used magic words and were kind. Treating parents this way is easy! Just remember to show them respect. What good manners have you practiced with your parents lately?

Amazing Facts about Manners with Parents

Parents and Names

What kids call their parents varies in different cultures. Kids in a Native American tribe in Arizona use "mother" for their mom and aunts. In a tribe in central Africa, "mother" and "father" are used for all adults in a community. In the United States, most kids call their parents a version of "mom" or "dad." But some kids call their parents by their first name instead! This does not show bad manners—as long as parents are okay with it.

Setting an Example

Good manners should be practiced your entire life. Adults should use good manners with their kids. This sets a good example. By seeing your parents use good manners with you, you will be more likely to use them, too! You can practice good manners as a family. Everyone should use magic words and be kind and polite.

Top Five Tips for Good Manners with Parents

1. Treat parents with respect.
2. Listen to parents' rules.
3. Follow parents' directions.
4. Be kind.
5. Don't forget to say "please" and "thank you!"

Glossary

appreciate — to recognize and be thankful for something.

consideration — careful thought before taking action.

permission — words or actions that tell someone it is okay to do something.

polite — showing good manners by the way you act or speak.

rude — showing bad manners by the way you act or speak.

situation — the event of a certain moment.

Web Sites

To learn more about manners, visit ABDO Group online at **www.abdopublishing.com**. Web sites about manners are featured on our Book Links page. These links are routinely monitored and updated to provide the most current information available.

Index